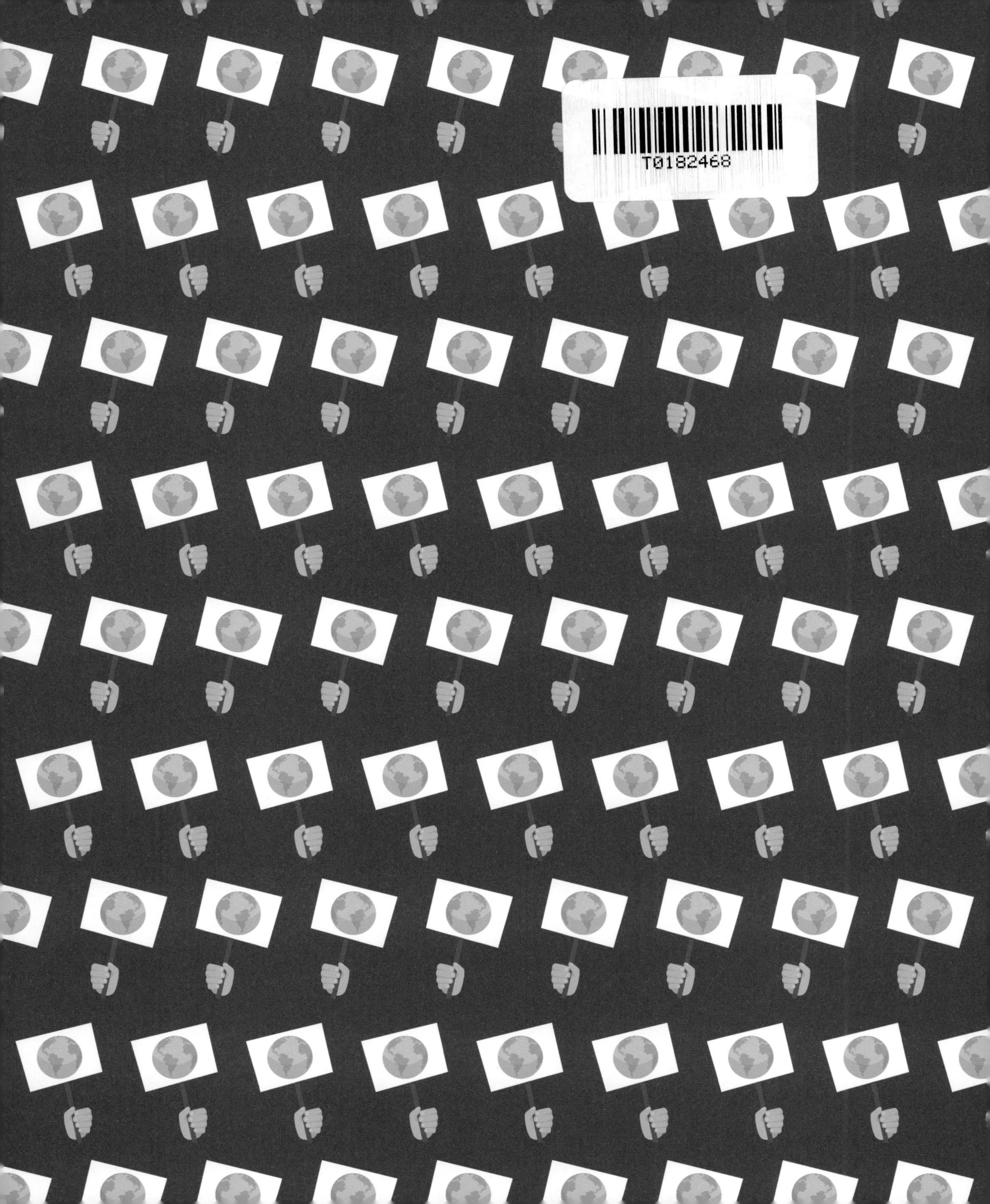

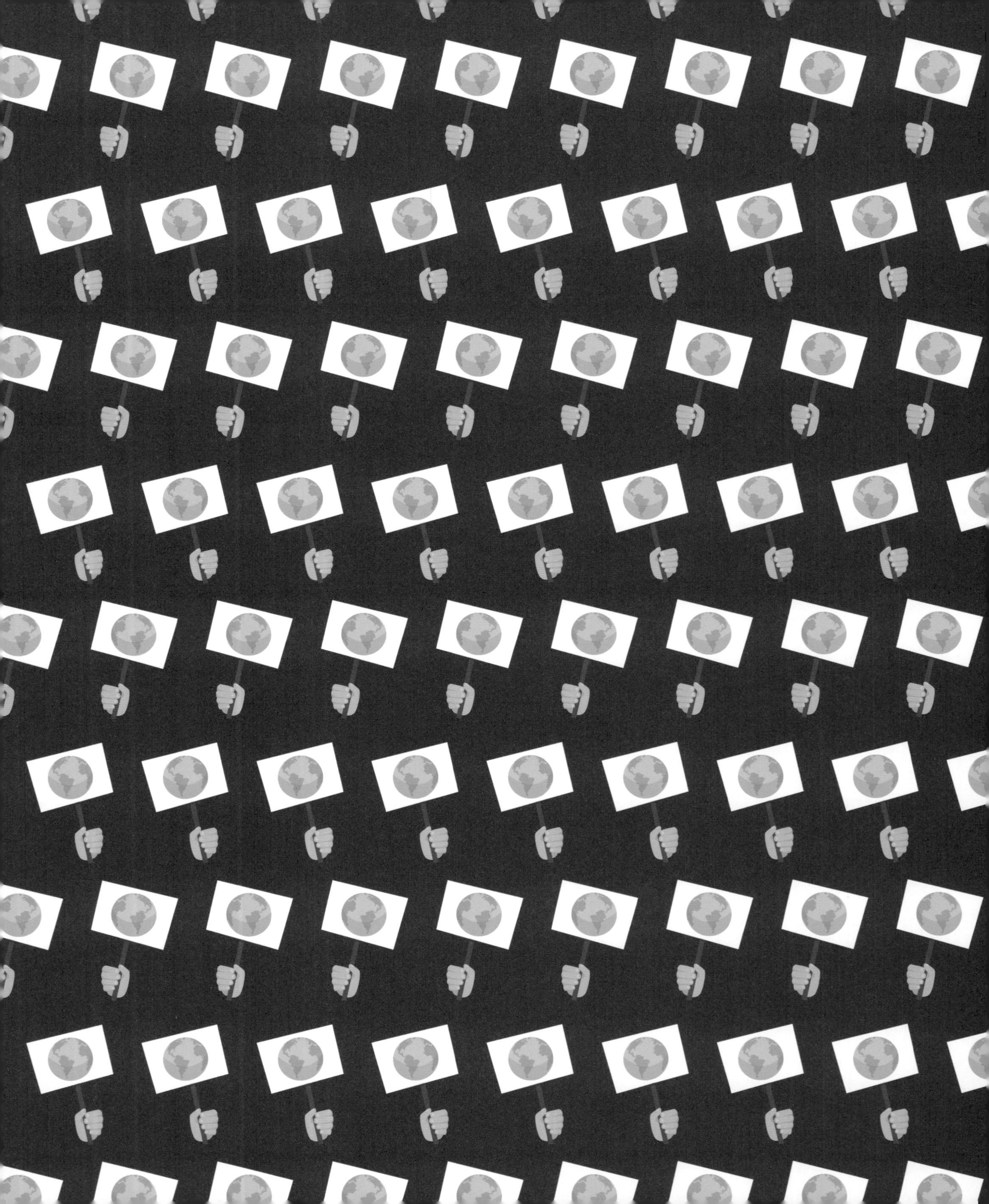

GRETA THUNBERG

GREAT LIVES IN GRAPHICS

Button
BOOKS

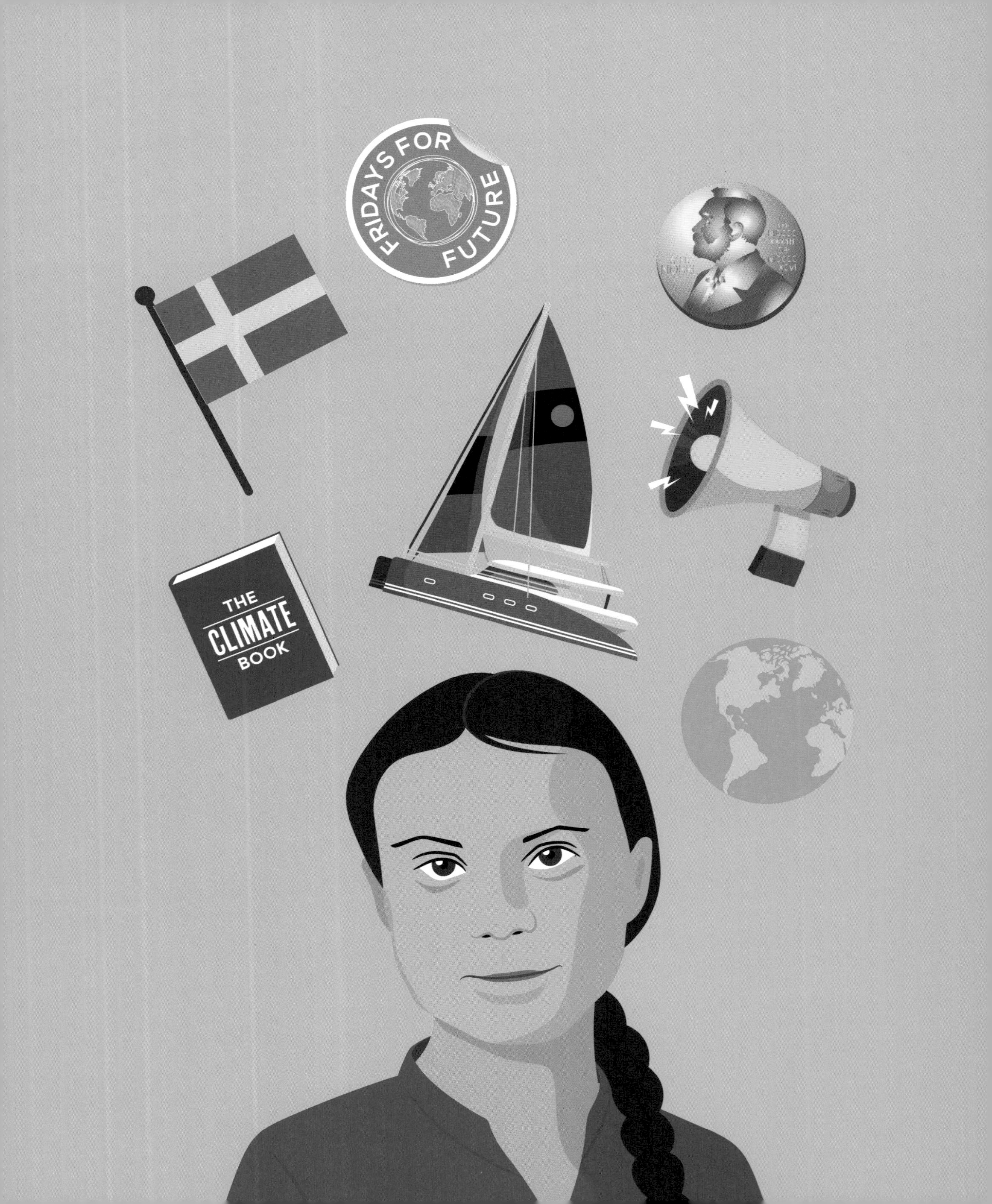
FRIDAYS FOR FUTURE
THE CLIMATE BOOK

Greta Thunberg is an environmental activist from Sweden whose attention-grabbing protests and inspirational speeches have made her one of the most famous faces of the modern green movement. Her Fridays for Future climate strikes have helped to kickstart a global wave of organised action involving young people designed to raise awareness about the dangers of global warming and to put pressure on the corporations and governments responsible.

But there's more to Greta's story. She has spoken out about living with Asperger syndrome, shining a light on the condition and how it can be a source of strength. Her long and gruelling voyages on zero-carbon yachts have also made people think about some of the sacrifices we all need to make to help tackle rising global temperatures. And like all brilliant people who change the world, she's made a few high-profile enemies along the way! Welcome to the radical and revolutionary world of Greta Thunberg…

GRETA'S WORLD

2009
Avatar, a film with a strong environmental message, becomes the biggest box office hit of all time

2003
Greta Thunberg is born in Stockholm, Sweden

2008
Barack Obama elected President of the United States

2012
Rover Curiosity takes a selfie on Mars

2006
Twitter is launched

2007
First iPhone is released

2015
The landmark Paris Agreement sees world leaders set long-term goals to limit global temperature increase to under 2°C this century

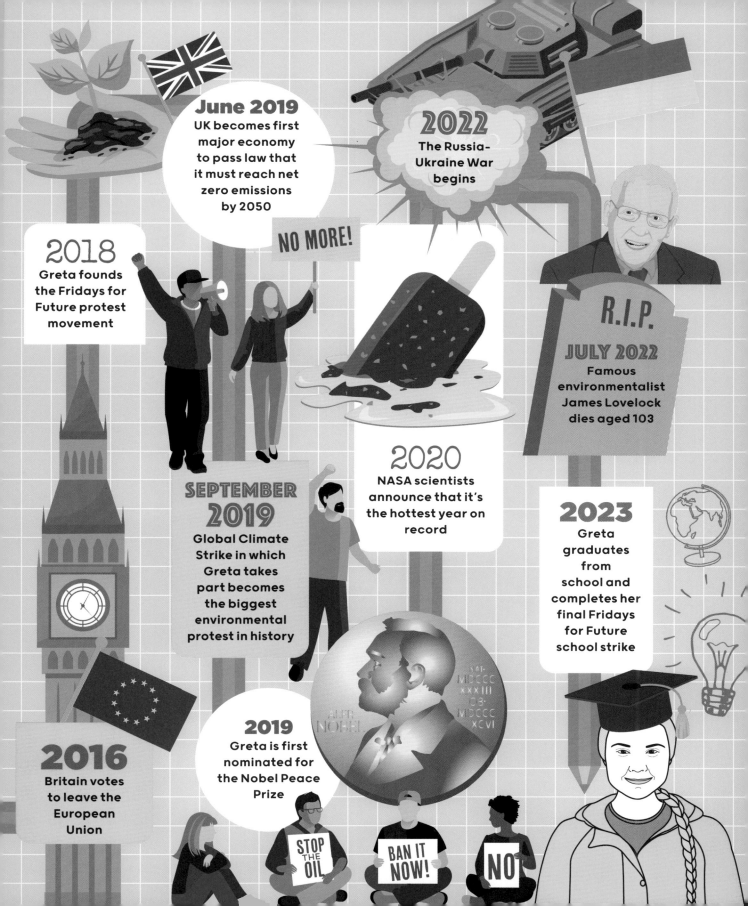

June 2019
UK becomes first major economy to pass law that it must reach net zero emissions by 2050

2022
The Russia-Ukraine War begins

2018
Greta founds the Fridays for Future protest movement

NO MORE!

R.I.P.

JULY 2022
Famous environmentalist James Lovelock dies aged 103

2020
NASA scientists announce that it's the hottest year on record

SEPTEMBER 2019
Global Climate Strike in which Greta takes part becomes the biggest environmental protest in history

2023
Greta graduates from school and completes her final Fridays for Future school strike

2016
Britain votes to leave the European Union

2019
Greta is first nominated for the Nobel Peace Prize

STOP THE OIL

BAN IT NOW!

NO

Greta

Greta Thunberg has become one of the most iconic figures of the early 21st century. It's no surprise that she should have stood out from the crowd, since her family is filled with Swedish stars that break the norm

Born: 3 JANUARY, 2003

Her hometown: STOCKHOLM, CAPITAL CITY OF SWEDEN

SWEDEN

STOCKHOLM

Stockholm facts

- First established as a town in 1252AD
- Built across parts of the Swedish mainland and a series of islands
- Often called one of the most beautiful cities in the world
- Cultural and scientific centre of Sweden

Her parents

Malena Ernman, OPERA SINGER

Her sister

Svante Thunberg, ACTOR & AUTHOR

Malena was Sweden's 2009 contestant for the Eurovision Song Contest.

Beata Thunberg, SINGER

Expectations

Her grandfather

Olof Thunberg, **ACTOR AND DIRECTOR**

Olof was the voice of a famous Swedish cartoon character called Bamse – a brown bear who becomes very strong by eating special honey. He also voiced the villainous tiger Shere Khan in the Swedish dubbed version of Disney's *The Jungle Book* cartoon.

Keep it in the family

Greta and her parents started to research and discuss the science behind climate change while she was a child. Greta's passion for the environment inspired her parents to make changes to their lifestyles. Svante became a vegan and Malena stopped travelling on planes for work.

VEGAN FOOD

Family matters

Greta has spoken about how she suffered from depression as a child, experiencing bullying at school and, for a while, refusing to speak. She was diagnosed with Asperger syndrome while at school. Her father Svante paused his career to become a fulltime carer for Greta and her sister during this difficult period. Svante and Malena published a book about it in 2018 called *Our House Is on Fire: Scenes of a Family and a Planet in Crisis*.

OUR HOUSE IS ON FIRE

GREEN ENERGY

Fridays for future

Having become deeply concerned with climate change, Greta searched for a way to make a greater impact in raising awareness around the issue. When the Swedish general election arrived in late 2018, she saw an opportunity...

Small beginnings

During the three weeks in August and September running up to the election, **Greta missed school to sit outside Sweden's parliament building** with a sign reading 'Skolstrejk för Klimatet' (School Strike for Climate). Initially she was on her own, but soon more and more people started to join her, drawing media coverage for the cause. They demanded that Sweden and other governments take urgent action on the climate crisis.

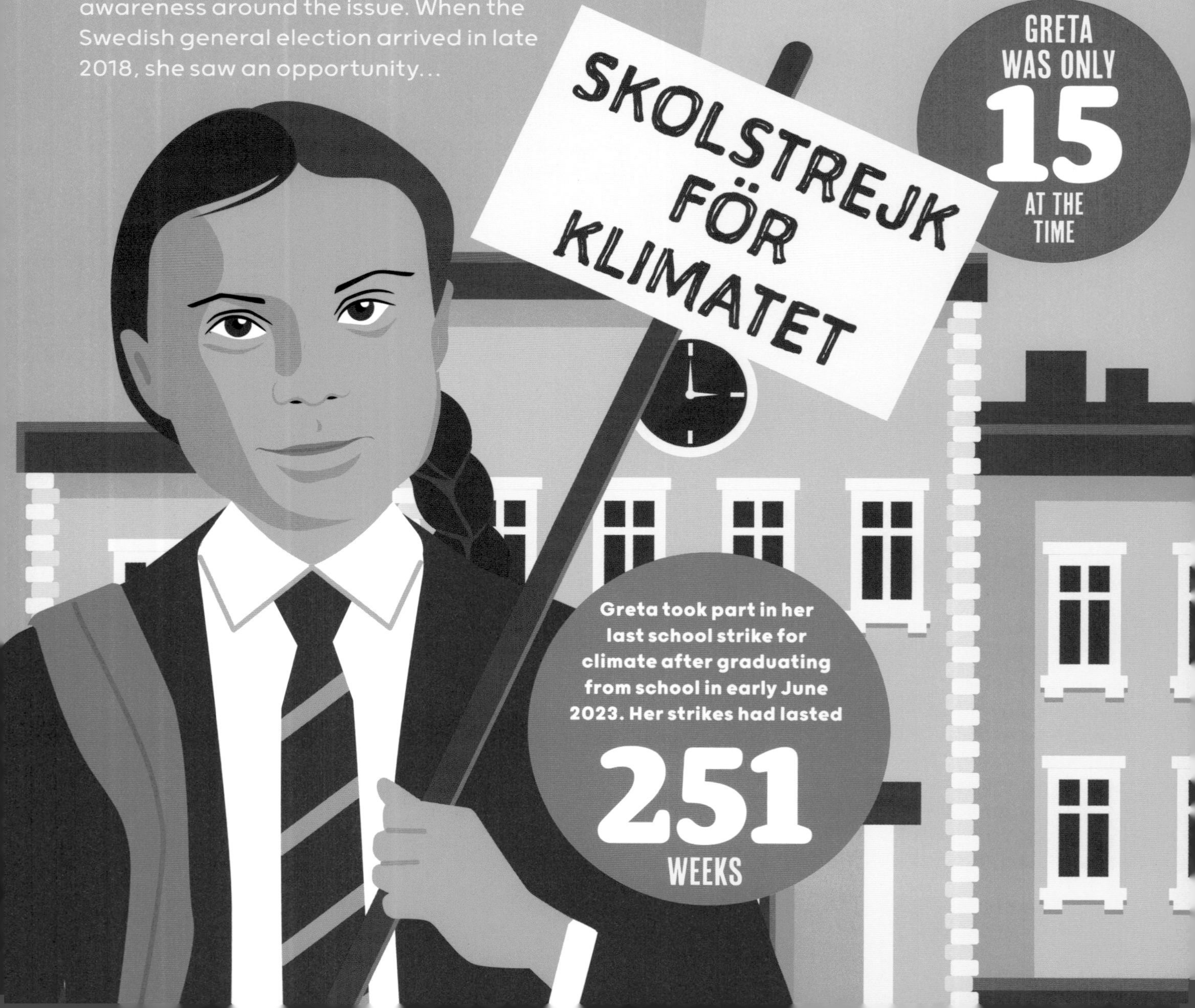
SKOLSTREJK
FÖR
KLIMATET

GRETA WAS ONLY **15** AT THE TIME

Greta took part in her last school strike for climate after graduating from school in early June 2023. Her strikes had lasted

251 WEEKS

Keep on going

After the election was over, Greta didn't give up. Every Friday, she continued to skip school to go on climate strike. She stated that she would continue to protest until the **Swedish government** showed that it had a pathway to reducing the country's **fossil fuel emissions** that would help keep global temperature rises under 2°C, in line with the **Paris Agreement**. These Fridays became known as Fridays for Future and her ongoing protest gained international attention.

What is the Paris Agreement?

A legally binding agreement entered into by 193 states, plus the countries of the European Union, vowing to reduce greenhouse gas emissions to limit the long-term effects of climate change.

A positive influence

Thousands of students around the world were inspired by Greta's Friday school strikes to carry out their own in the months and years since. Fridays for Future have happened in…

USA · UK · FRANCE

BELGIUM · NETHERLANDS

DENMARK · PERU

CANADA · SIERRA LEONE

BANGLADESH

SCHOOL STRIKE FOR CLIMATE!

They've taken place in…

7,500 CITIES

on EVERY CONTINENT

WITH MORE THAN 14m PEOPLE

TRUTH TELLER

What was COP24?

The 2018 United Nations Climate Change Conference in Katowice, Poland. Beginning in 1995, a conference is held annually in which world leaders meet to discuss progress in fighting the causes of manmade climate change. Every conference is held in a different country, including:

 1995 Berlin, Germany

 1997 Kyoto, Japan

 2006 Nairobi, Kenya

2021 Glasgow, UK

 2023 Dubai, UAE

Public platform

At COP24 in Poland in December 2018, Greta gave an explosive speech in which she called out the dishonesty and slowness of the participating countries:

'You are not mature enough to tell it like it is. Even that burden you leave to us children. But I don't care about being popular. I care about... the living planet.'

157 2766 373

'Our biosphere is being sacrificed so that rich people in countries like mine can live in luxury. It is the sufferings of the many which pay for the luxuries of the few.'

921 7307 126

 SAVE OUR PLANET

Soon after the Fridays for Future strikes started, Greta began to receive invitations to speak at international events about climate change. Her outspoken and passionate comments went viral online and Greta quickly became a figurehead for the youth environmentalist movement

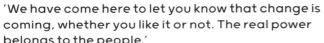

'We need to keep the fossil fuels in the ground, and we need to focus on equity. And if solutions within the system are so impossible to find, maybe we should change the system itself.'

❤ 791 💬 8101 🔁 64

'We have come here to let you know that change is coming, whether you like it or not. The real power belongs to the people.'

Going viral

Greta's angry, passionate speeches were shared millions of times across social media platforms, further raising awareness among young people globally about the urgency for action on climate change.

 5.6 mil
X/Twitter followers

 14.7 mil
Instagram followers

❤ 812 💬 9412 🔁 126

Truth to power

Greta generated even more headlines – and ruffled even more feathers! – during a speech she gave at the **UN Climate Action Summit in New York on 23 September, 2019**, where she criticised state leaders, lawmakers and the UN Secretary-General:

'You have stolen my dreams and my childhood with your empty words. And yet I'm one of the lucky ones. People are suffering. People are dying. Entire ecosystems are collapsing… We are in the beginning of a mass extinction, and all you can talk about is money and fairy tales of eternal economic growth. How dare you!'

❤ 799 💬 9110 ⚫ 754

OCEAN ODYSSEY

When she was invited to speak at the UN Climate Action Summit in New York, Greta knew she couldn't break her rule against flying to get there. Instead, she took to the Atlantic Ocean in the *Malizia II* zero-emission yacht for a fantastic voyage...

SET SAIL FROM PLYMOUTH, ENGLAND

UK

USA

ARRIVED IN NEW YORK ON 28 AUGUST, 2019

THE JOURNEY TOOK OVER 2 WEEKS

ATLANTIC OCEAN

PORTUGAL

DEPARTED HAMPTON, VIRGINIA ON 13 NOVEMBER

3,500 NAUTICAL MILE JOURNEY DURING HURRICANE SEASON

ARRIVED IN LISBON ON 3 DECEMBER

····· **OUTWARD JOURNEY**

····· **RETURN JOURNEY**

RETURN JOURNEY

Greta made her voyage back to Europe aboard the catamaran *La Vagabonde*, departing from Hampton, Virginia on 13 November and arriving in Lisbon, Portugal on 3 December.

WHAT IS A CATAMARAN?

A type of watercraft with **two parallel hulls**

GRETA'S DIET

onboard was freeze-dried vegan meals

BOAT BUDDIES

Greta travelled with her father, a cameraman and a two-man supporting crew.

THE **MALIZIA II** YACHT

HIGH-SPEED PLANING MONOHULL

BUILT FOR 2016-2017 SINGLE-HANDED, NON-STOP, ROUND-THE-WORLD VENDÉE GLOBE RACE

18 METRES LONG

NO TOILETS OR SHOWERS - ONLY BLUE BUCKETS!

USES **UNDERWATER TURBINES** TO GENERATE ELECTRICITY FROM ZERO-CARBON HYDROPOWER

PROPELLED BY **THE WIND**

USES **SOLAR PANELS** ON DECK TO GENERATE POWER FOR COMMUNICATIONS AND LIGHTING

ONBOARD LAB TO MEASURE OCEAN SURFACE CO_2 AND WATER TEMPERATURE

ECO-TOURISM

Greta's sea voyages boosted interest in alternative travel options among tourists keen to avoid enlarging their carbon footprint via air travel. Travel agencies cashed in by creating new sea journey holidays on cargo ships and sailing vessels.

OBAMA

In the US, Greta met the former US President Barack Obama and spoke to the House Foreign Affairs Committee and the House Select Committee in Washington DC.

MAKING HISTORY

Shortly after arriving in New York, Greta took part in the largest climate protest in history on the streets of the iconic city and around the world

THE GLOBAL CLIMATE STRIKE

An expansion of the youth climate activism started by Greta in 2018, the Global Climate Strike or Global Week for Future involved millions of people in dozens of countries uniting to protest against the fossil fuel emissions and pollutions carried out by governments worldwide.

DATE:
20-27 SEPTEMBER, 2019

4-6 MILLION PEOPLE GLOBALLY

250,000 PEOPLE IN NEW YORK

PARTICIPANTS INCLUDED:
* MEMBERS OF TRADE UNIONS
* WORKERS FROM COMPANIES LIKE AMAZON & GOOGLE
* DOCTORS & NURSES
* STUDENTS

ACT NOW OR WE WILL!

The strike began in the **Pacific Islands**, where protesters took part in protests, poetry readings and discussions centred around demands that world governments do more to address rising sea levels that are affecting the islands and their inhabitants.

300,000 people took part in 100 street rallies in **Australia**, protesting the country's massive export industry of oil and gas.

Hundreds of students and environmental activists marched in Tokyo and other cities in **Japan**.

RESPECT EXISTENCE OR EXPECT RESISTANCE!

In Nairobi, **Kenya's** capital city, protesters wore costumes made from plastic bottles to highlight the dangers of plastic waste for people living in developing countries.

UNITED BEHIND THE SCIENCE!

Education chiefs in **New York** gave the 1.1 million children in their schools permission to attend the strike. In New York, Greta spoke at a rally outside the United Nations headquarters.

In **Thailand**, hundreds of young people fell to the ground outside the environment ministry in Bangkok, pretending to have died in order to draw attention to the serious consequences of climate change breakdown.

Protesters in Delhi in **India** focused on the terrible air pollution issue in the city.

In Kabul in **Afghanistan**, around 100 young protesters were protected by an armoured personnel carrier as they marched.

SOLO STRIKES

In **Russia**, where almost all protest is illegal and prevented by the government, individuals took part in solo strikes. People in queues would take it in turns to hold up a placard for five minute intervals.

CLIMATE CRISIS

What exactly is climate change, how are humans causing it and why does it matter?

WEATHER V CLIMATE

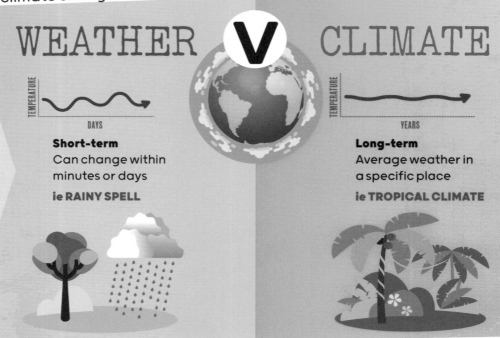

Weather is what happens on a day-to-day basis and it's constantly changing. It might be rainy in the morning, but sunny in the afternoon.

Climate describes how the usual weather conditions in an area change over long periods of time - decades or even longer.

TEMPERATURE
DAYS

Short-term
Can change within minutes or days
ie RAINY SPELL

TEMPERATURE
YEARS

Long-term
Average weather in a specific place
ie TROPICAL CLIMATE

WHAT CONTROLS THE CLIMATE?

Climate change is the process of Earth's temperature changing over long periods of time. Naturally occurring greenhouse gases, such as carbon dioxide (CO_2), methane, nitrous oxide and water vapour have been part of the Earth's climate throughout history. In the past, these gases surrounded the planet, trapped heat from the Sun and kept Earth at the right temperature for life to thrive.

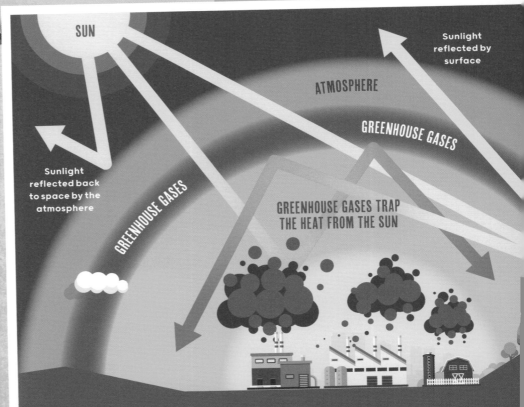

SUN

Sunlight reflected by surface

ATMOSPHERE

GREENHOUSE GASES

Sunlight reflected back to space by the atmosphere

GREENHOUSE GASES

GREENHOUSE GASES TRAP THE HEAT FROM THE SUN

EARTH HAS BECOME AROUND 1°C WARMER IN THE LAST 150 YEARS

ENVIRONMENTAL EFFECTS

Scientists predict that the long-term effects of climate change will affect the lives of people and animals all over the world as they find it harder to adapt to the changing climate.

Weather woes
The weather will become more extreme and unpredictable, including:

FLOODING

HEAT WAVES

WILDFIRES

DROUGHTS

SEVERE STORMS

Meltdown
Climate change is also warming the oceans, causing our planet's sea ice and glaciers to melt, which will make sea levels rise, threatening coastal communities and animals like polar bears that live on the ice at the poles.

THE GREENHOUSE EFFECT

Scientists believe human activities are upsetting the balance by releasing extra greenhouse gases, such as CO_2 and methane. Manmade climate change is the result of things humans do, including burning fossil fuels – such as oil, coal and natural gas – large-scale farming and deforestation (cutting down forests that absorb greenhouse gases). All of these activities allow more greenhouse gas to enter the atmosphere where they trap more heat from the Sun and start to make things dangerously warm.

Sunlight absorbed at the surface

POLLUTION PROBLEM

Climate change isn't the only environmental problem caused by humans. We're also responsible for polluting our planet by releasing harmful substances into our air, soil and water, such as:

SEWAGE
Poo, wee and gross stuff flushed down toilets and drains

PESTICIDES
Chemicals used to kill insects and weeds to protect crops

WASTE PRODUCTS
From factories, such as smoke and toxic chemicals

Pollution is creating issues like:

AIR POLLUTION
Damaging people's health and right to breathe clean air

ACID RAIN
Killing trees and animal life in rivers, lakes and oceans

Stimulating the growth of cyanobacteria that feed on waste products and kill other forms of aquatic life

Planet protest

Campaign groups like Greenpeace, Extinction Rebellion and Just Stop Oil are using attention-grabbing protests and social media messaging to put pressure on political leaders and persuade ordinary people that the climate situation is serious and urgent.

Help or hindrance?

Some of these groups are controversial, with critics saying that their **disruptive tactics** put off 'ordinary' people and risk overshadowing their climate message. Others argue that such actions are justified and necessary to raise awareness because of the climate emergency. **What do you think?**

EXTINCTION REBELLION WANT:

THE DECLARATION OF A 'CLIMATE EMERGENCY' BY THE GOVERNMENT

A LEGAL COMMITMENT TO NET ZERO CARBON EMISSIONS BY 2025 IN THE UK

THE CREATION OF A CITIZENS' ASSEMBLY TO OVERSEE THE PROCESS

JUST STOP OIL WANT:

A HALT TO NEW LICENSES FOR NEW FOSSIL FUEL PROJECTS IN THE UK

Protecting

What is net zero?

It means cutting manmade **greenhouse gas emissions** to as close to zero as possible in order to keep rising global temperatures under control. In 2015, **195 countries signed up to the landmark Paris Agreement** to limit global warming to **below 2°C** by moving towards net-zero carbon targets by **2050**.

The agreement works on a **five-year cycle,** with countries expected to reveal increasingly ambitious plans for emissions reductions towards the end of each period. However, many activist groups do not think that governments are moving fast enough or with ambitious enough targets to meet the 2050 deadline.

Green machines

One of the most important parts of moving towards a low carbon-emission future is replacing fossil fuels with renewable energy sources.

RENEWABLE: drawn from a natural source that can be restored at a higher rate than it's used.

FOSSIL FUELS: not renewable, because it takes hundreds of millions of years for new coal, oil and gas to form, so they're used quicker than they can be replaced.

TACTICS

GLUING OR TYING THEMSELVES TO BUILDINGS AND WORKS OF ART

INTERRUPTING HIGH-PROFILE PUBLIC EVENTS

BLOCKING ROADS BY SITTING OR STANDING IN THEM

Renewable energy sources

WIND POWER
Wind turns the turbines and electricity is generated

SOLAR POWER
Special photovoltaic panels and mirrors capture sunlight and convert it into electricity

HYDROPOWER
Dams are built to control the flow of water. When water is released, it flows down the dam through a turbine, powering a generator and creating electricity

our planet!

The experts agree there's a problem, but what can be done about it? Scientists, activist groups and individuals like Greta are busy raising awareness about climate change's alarming effects and pushing for solutions that will reduce or even reverse its impact...

Fossil fuels are made from:

The fossilised remains of **decomposing** plants and animals from **millions of years ago, stored in the Earth's crust.** They contain carbon and hydrogen which can be used to generate heat and produce energy.

GEOTHERMAL POWER
The heat energy from inside the Earth is tapped from geothermal reservoirs - wells of water naturally heated by the planet

ENTER THE

His ideas about living simply and close to **nature,** as well as learning to **appreciate the animal and plant life** of the natural world, remain central to environmentalism to this day.

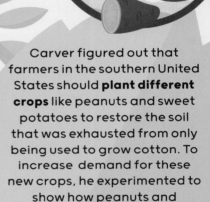

Carver figured out that farmers in the southern United States should **plant different crops** like peanuts and sweet potatoes to restore the soil that was exhausted from only being used to grow cotton. To increase demand for these new crops, he experimented to show how peanuts and sweet potatoes could be used to make:

BORN INTO SLAVERY. ATTENDED UNIVERSITY LATER IN LIFE & EARNED A MASTER'S DEGREE IN AGRICULTURAL SCIENCE.

MILK

RUBBER

PLASTICS

INK

SOAP

Henry David Thoreau
(1817–1862)
WRITER & PHILOSOPHER

George Washington Carver (1861–1943)
AGRICULTURAL CHEMIST & EXPERIMENTER

AND MUCH MORE!

Thoreau's account of the two years he spent living alone in the **American wilderness in a cabin** beside a pond, *Walden; or Life in the Woods*, remains one of the most famous environmentalist books ever written.

His ideas helped to raise **awareness** about the importance of crop diversification and soil conservation.

WALDEN

INITIALLY *WALDEN* TOOK 5 YEARS TO SELL JUST 2000 COPIES. IT IS NOW TAUGHT IN SCHOOLS

ENVIRONMENTALISTS

Environmentalism has a long and lively history. Let's take a look at some of its most innovative and important thinkers…

In *The Vanishing Face of Gaia: A Final Warning* (2009) Lovelock warned that **manmade climate** change was a **major threat to the Earth system.**

Often considered the founder of the **modern environmentalist movement.** Wrote many books about the ocean, including the bestselling *The Sea Around Us*. Carson published *Silent Spring* in 1962, a controversial popular science book that informed ordinary people about the seriously harmful environmental effects of **pesticides**. Carson's ideas were proven to be correct and commonly used pesticides like DDT were banned.

THE SEA AROUND US

SILENT SPRING

2 MILLION COPIES SOLD

James Lovelock
(1919-2022)
CHEMIST, INVENTOR & AUTHOR

Rachel Carson
(1907-1964)
BIOLOGIST

Her ideas about manmade pollution pushing the natural world towards collapse were massively influential on **modern environmentalism**.

Came up with the **Gaia hypothesis:** the idea that the whole of planet Earth, including all its lifeforms, is a self-regulating organism or system. Gaia has come to be accepted by many scientists as a way of thinking about how the **complex relationships** between Earth's organisms can be affected by human activities, like climate change.

WORKED FOR NASA AND MI5!

Greta

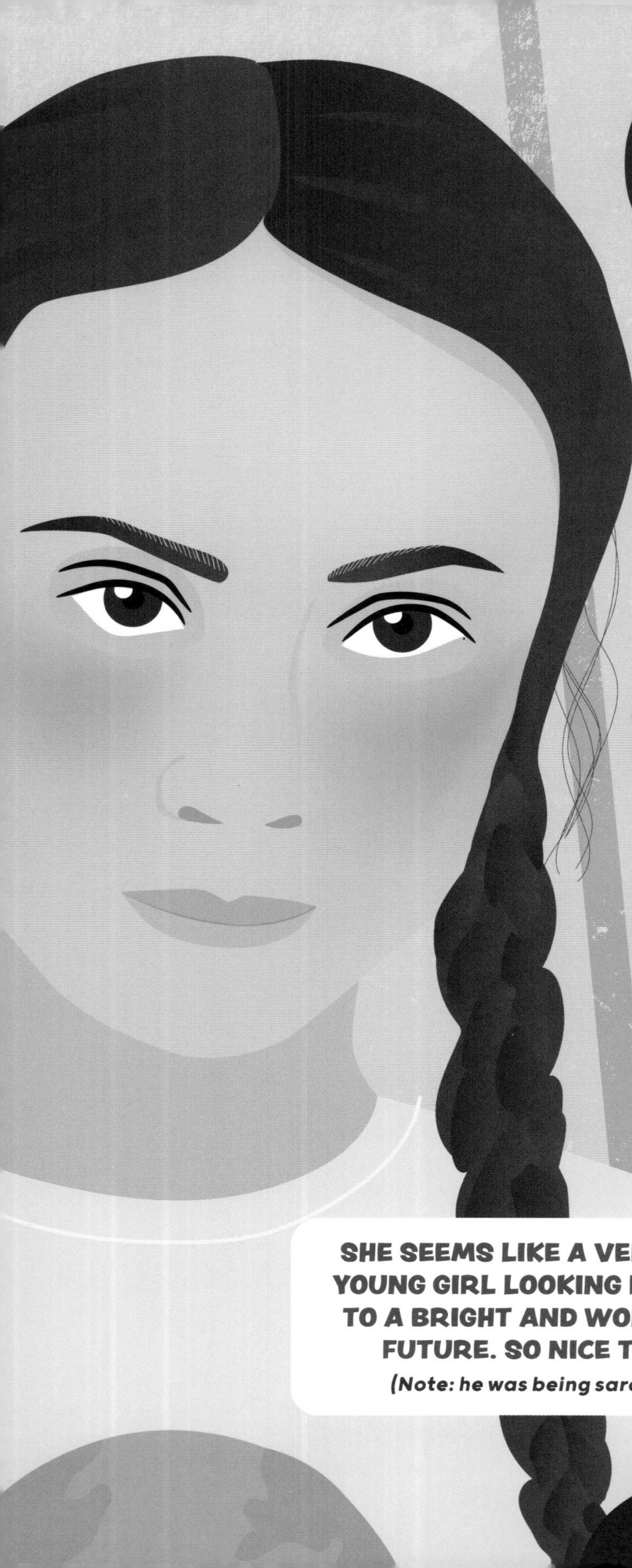

DONALD TRUMP (1946-)

45TH PRESIDENT OF THE UNITED STATES, BUSINESSMAN AND MEDIA PERSONALITY

A long-term critic of climate science and the green movement, Trump carried out a range of anti-environmental actions after being elected as president in 2017, including:

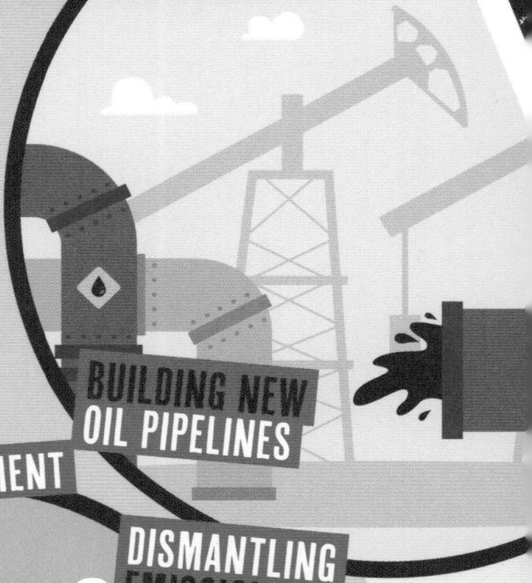

- BUILDING NEW OIL PIPELINES
- WITHDRAWING THE US FROM THE PARIS AGREEMENT
- DISMANTLING EMISSIONS REGULATIONS
- LIFTING BANS ON OIL AND GAS EXPLORATION

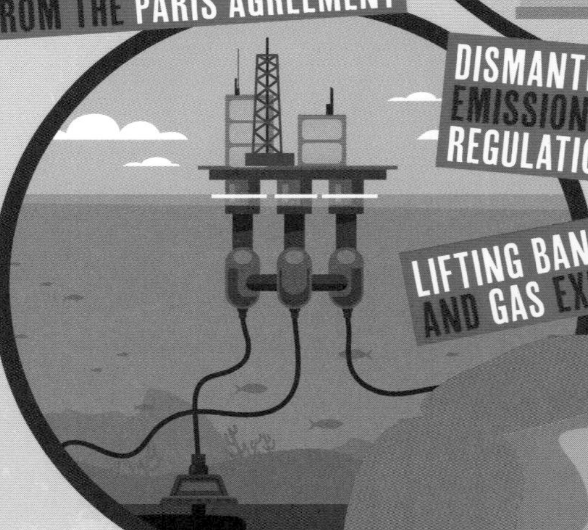

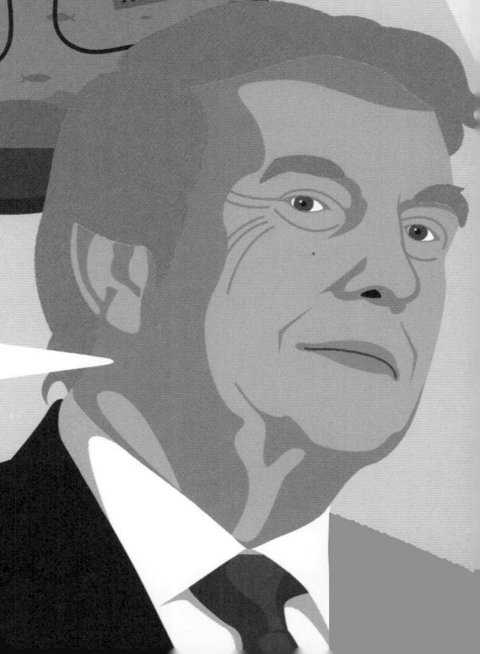

SHE SEEMS LIKE A VERY HAPPY YOUNG GIRL LOOKING FORWARD TO A BRIGHT AND WONDERFUL FUTURE. SO NICE TO SEE!

(Note: he was being sarcastic!)

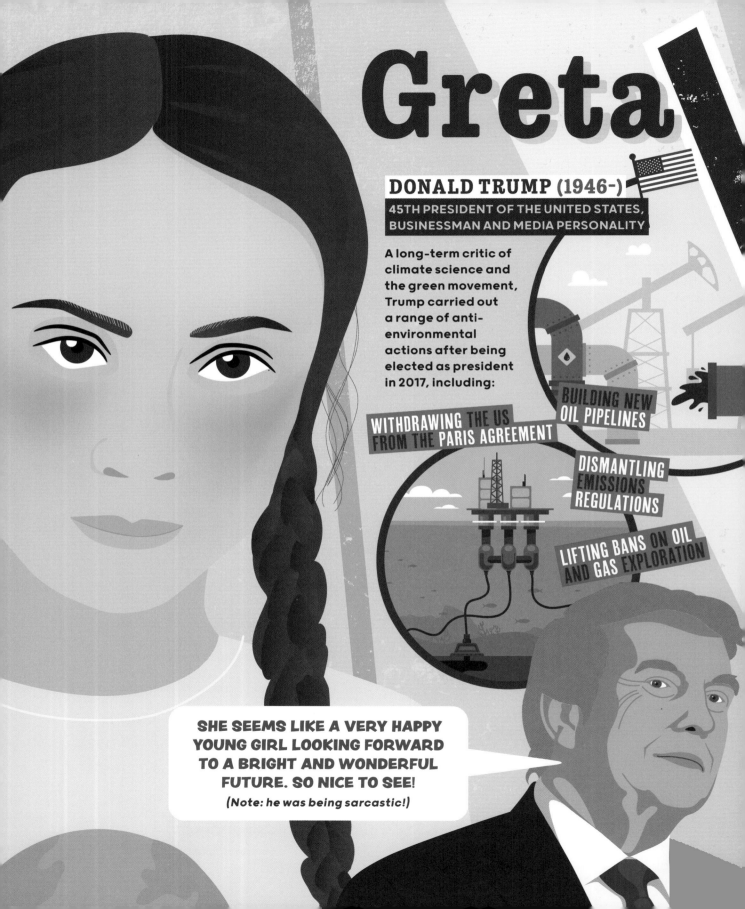

Politicians

Greta has won over millions of ordinary people, but she's also made some enemies among the world's most controversial political leaders...

JAIR BOLSONARO (1955-)
PRESIDENT OF BRAZIL & MILITARY OFFICER

A right-wing, nationalist politician, Bolsonaro pursued an anti-environmental agenda during his time as Brazil's president from 2019 to 2023, including:

FAILING TO PROTECT THE INDIGENOUS PEOPLE OF THE AMAZON

REDUCING THE POWERS OF BRAZIL'S ENVIRONMENTAL AGENCIES

ALLOWING MAJOR DEFORESTATION OF THE AMAZON RAINFOREST

> IT'S AMAZING HOW MUCH SPACE THE PRESS GIVES THIS BRAT.

VLADIMIR PUTIN (1952-)
PRESIDENT OF RUSSIA & FORMER INTELLIGENCE OFFICER

Putin's views on climate science seem to have shifted over time and are hard to pin down. Initially he suggested that humans were not responsible for climate change, but in recent years he has implied in his public statements that fossil fuel emissions are to blame. He has made pledges to drastically reduce Russia's emissions, but so far few practical changes have been made and Russia's economy remains heavily dependent on the sale of fossil fuels abroad.

> NOBODY EXPLAINED TO GRETA THAT THE MODERN WORLD IS COMPLICATED AND COMPLEX.

'ECOCIDE'

In 2023 there were reports that Russia was behind the destruction of a large dam under their control in Ukraine, causing massive flooding, the evacuation of thousands of people and enormous environmental damage. Greta condemned the incident and said that Russia should be punished for the 'ecocide' they were carrying out as part of their war in the Ukraine.

SUPERPOWER

After being diagnosed with Asperger syndrome, which is now considered a type of autism, Greta described it as her 'superpower', giving her a unique outlook on the world that sets her apart from others...

THE SYNDROME IS NAMED AFTER AUSTRIAN PHYSICIAN **HANS ASPERGER**, WHO FIRST IDENTIFIED ITS SYMPTOMS IN 1944. THE NAME IS NOW CONTROVERSIAL BECAUSE HANS IS KNOWN TO HAVE COLLABORATED WITH NAZI AUTHORITIES BEFORE AND DURING WORLD WAR TWO.

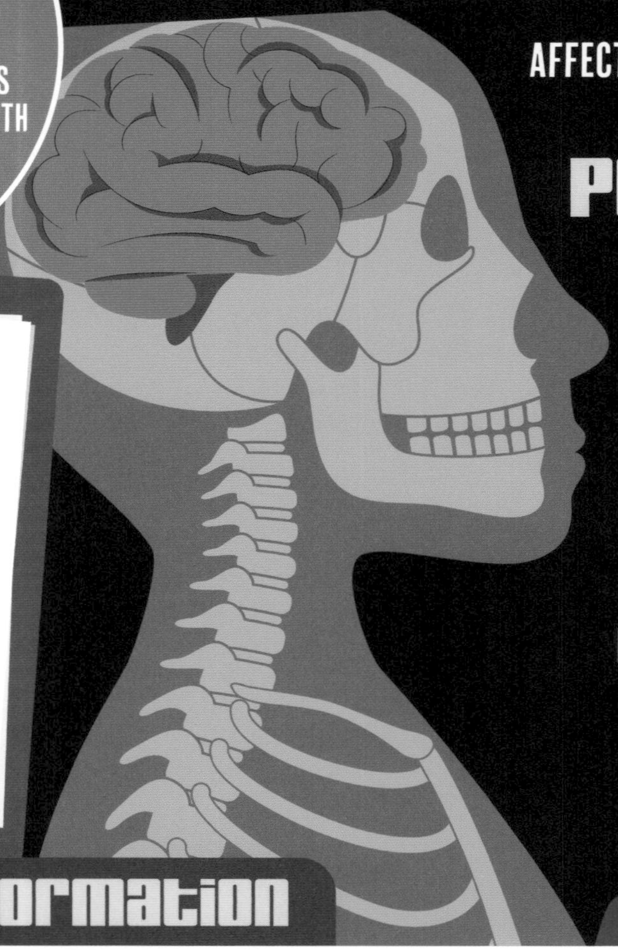

AFFECTS APPROXIMATELY **37M PEOPLE** GLOBALLY

3-4 TIMES MORE COMMON IN BOYS THAN GIRLS

Symptoms can include:

- REPETITIVE BEHAVIOUR
- AVOIDING EYE CONTACT
- DIFFICULTY WITH SOCIAL INTERACTION
- CAN APPEAR PHYSICALLY CLUMSY
- STRONG OR EVEN OBSESSIVE INTEREST IN A SINGLE SUBJECT
- ANXIETY OR DEPRESSION

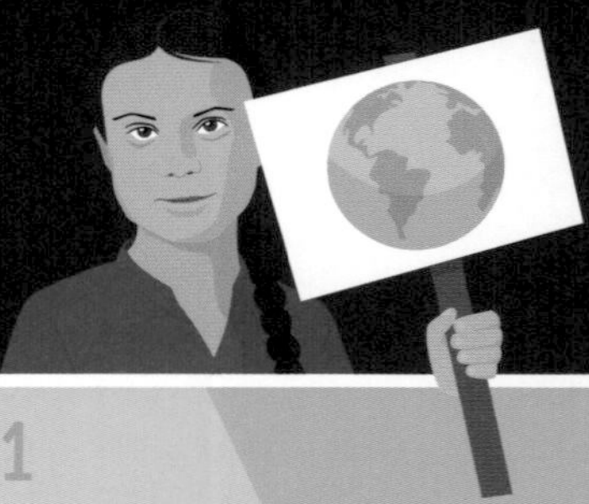

GRETA'S TRANSFORMATION

AGE 8
Learns about climate change, over the next few years becomes vegan and refuses to travel by plane.

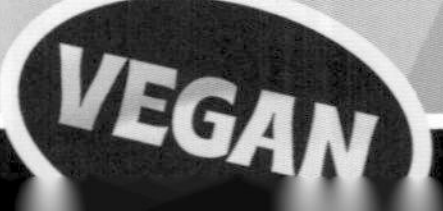
VEGAN

AGE 10
Badly bullied at school, Greta describes herself as 'that girl in the back who never said anything'.

AGE 11
Greta is near-mute - she doesn't speak to anyone outside her family for three years.

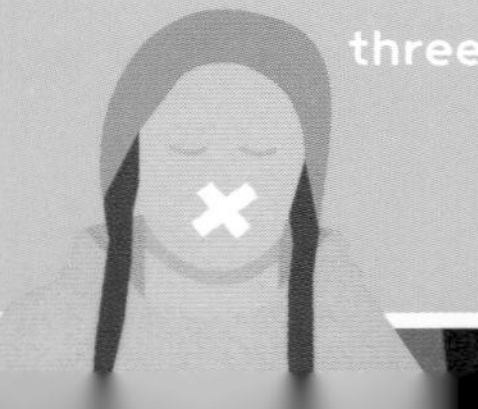

AGE 15
Begins protesting outside the Swedish parliament.

1 Unlike people with autism, those with Asperger syndrome **do not usually** have learning difficulties or problems with their speech.

2 It can be difficult to **diagnose** Asperger syndrome and a person can have it for many years without realising it. When identified, it can be **treated** with methods aimed at improving a patient's social and communication skills and their physical coordination.

3 Greta's condition has likely played a role in her single-minded **determination** to fight for climate justice, and by talking openly about it she has also helped to **decrease the stigma** and prejudice surrounding Asperger syndrome.

4 Many people with the condition can use their ability to **focus their attention on a single subject** to become leading experts in their chosen field and have highly successful careers.

'I HAVE **ASPERGER'S** AND THAT MEANS I'M SOMETIMES **a bit different** FROM THE NORM. AND – GIVEN THE RIGHT CIRCUMSTANCES – BEING DIFFERENT IS A **SUPERPOWER**'

OTHER FAMOUS NEURODIVERGENT PEOPLE

BILL GATES Billionaire businessman, co-founder of Windows software company (diagnosed with dyslexia and Attention Deficit Hyperactivity Disorder)

DANIEL RADCLIFFE The *Harry Potter* actor has been open about living with dyspraxia, a condition associated with poor physical coordination skills, as well as attention and memory problems

TEMPLE GRANDIN Animal behaviourist and academic who is also a spokesperson for autism

BILLIE EILISH The bestselling musical artist was diagnosed with Tourette's syndrome aged 11, a condition that causes a person to make involuntary sounds and movements

AGE 16 Speaks in front of 25,000 people in Berlin.

AGE 19 Moves into a flat in the centre of Stockholm.

AGE 20 Graduates from high school and attends last school strike for climate.

TODAY Greta hangs out with her best friends, who are also climate activists. They like to:
✔ Play games
✔ Enjoy *fika* (coffee and cake)
✔ Listen to Taylor Swift, My Chemical Romance, Swedish folk and punk music

Malala Yousafzai

Born in Mingora in Pakistan, Malala was an **outspoken critic** of the Islamic Taliban movement that took control of her home region in 2008 and began burning down girls' schools, preventing them from receiving an education. She **wrote a diary** that was published by the BBC in 2009 in which she emphasised the importance of **female education and freedom**. The **Taliban** targeted her and she survived being **shot in the head** on a school bus in 2012. She moved to England where she continues to speak on behalf of women's rights.

WINNER
2014 Nobel Peace Prize

IN 2013 NAMED 1 OF
100 most influential
PEOPLE IN THE WORLD
BY TIME MAGAZINE

BREAKING

ONE OF
TIME MAGAZINE'S
25 Most Influential
TEENS OF 2018

Thandiwe Abdullah

Taken to political rallies as a child by her mother, the American academic and civic leader Melina Abdullah, Thandiwe has chalked up an impressive list of successes as an **activist** in her own right. She became involved with the **Black Lives Matter** movement that is highlighting racism and discrimination against Black people in the United States and elsewhere, co-founding the BLM Youth Vanguard, helping to establish the Black Lives Matter in Schools programme and campaigning to end random police searches of students in LA schools.

ADDRESSED
500,000 people
AT THE 2018 WOMEN'S MARCH
IN LOS ANGELES

Iqbal Masih

Iqbal was a Pakistani Christian who was sold into **child labour** in a carpet factory as an infant. Escaping from his owner, he went on to become **a campaigner** against the abusive treatment of child labourers in his own country, speaking to international audiences. Tragically, he was assassinated at the age of 12, probably by men hired by the owners of the carpet factories that used child labour, but he remains an **important symbol** of the suffering of children forced into servitude worldwide.

Greta isn't the only person to achieve fame at a young age for activism. Here are some of the world's most important young revolutionaries, past and present, who weren't afraid to stand apart from the crowd or risk it all for what's right...

The Iqbal Masih Award
FOR THE ELIMINATION OF CHILD LABOUR IS PRESENTED EVERY YEAR BY THE US SECRETARY OF LABOUR

BARRIERS

Nkosi Johnson

Born with **Aids** in Johannesburg, South Africa, because his mother was HIV positive when pregnant with him, Nkosi was refused entry to a local primary school as a result of his condition. His case became a **political flashpoint** in the country, leading to changes in the law that made it illegal to discriminate against people with HIV. Nkosi began to campaign on behalf of other children with Aids, setting up **Nkosi's Haven**, an organisation supporting mothers and children affected by the disease. He became a key note speaker at the 2000 International Aids conference at the age of 11. Sadly, he died the following year.

The International Children's Peace Prize
WAS ESTABLISHED IN NKOSI'S MEMORY. IT IS GIVEN TO A CHILD WHO HAS MADE A SIGNIFICANT CONTRIBUTION TO CAMPAIGNING FOR CHILDREN'S RIGHTS AND SAFEGUARDING VULNERABLE CHILDREN.

Greta was named *Time* magazine's **PERSON OF THE YEAR** in 2019. She appeared on the cover and was profiled inside.

SCREEN QUEEN

Greta's activism has been immortalised onscreen in a 2020 documentary film called *I Am Greta* that premiered at the prestigious Venice International Film Festival and a 2021 BBC mini-series called *Greta Thunberg: A Year to Change the World.*

WHAT GRETA DID NEXT...

Greta has already made a massive contribution to the modern green movement, but she's not slowing down any time soon. In the last couple of years, she's kept up her activism and worked with scientists, writers and filmmakers to bring her story and the realities of the climate emergency to a wider audience

ARRESTED!

Greta has repeatedly been detained by the police while taking part in climate-related protests, including in Oslo, during protests against the construction of 151 wind turbines on land inhabited by the indigenous Sámi people of Arctic Norway, disrupting their way of life. And in London in October 2023, during a protest outside a meeting between fossil fuel executives and UK politicians.

MISS G THUNBERG

5 X NOMINEE FOR **NOBEL PEACE PRIZE** in 2019, 2020, 2021, 2022 and 2023

Winning a Nobel Prize is widely considered to be one of the greatest honours in the world. Set up by the Swedish inventor and businessman Alfred Nobel in his will and awarded annually since 1901, the six Nobel prizes are meant to reward people or teams who have done ground-breaking and world-changing work in…

PHYSICS **CHEMISTRY** MEDICINE **LITERATURE** PEACE-MAKING **ECONOMICS**

MASSIVE GRETA THUNBERG **MURALS** HAVE BEEN CREATED IN PLACES LIKE BRISTOL AND SAN FRANCISCO

BRISTOL MURAL
15M HIGH

SAN FRANCISCO MURAL
18M HIGH

NAME-DROPPING

Scientists have also named some newly discovered animal species in honour of Greta Thunberg and her work to protect the wonders of the natural world, including:

THUNBERGA GRETA
A species of huntsman spider from Madagascar.

NELLOPTODES GRETAE
A tiny species of beetle from East Africa measuring just 0.79mm that is pale yellow and gold in colour.

CRASPEDOTROPIS GRETATHUNBERGAE
A small species of snail found in Brunei.

THE CLIMATE BOOK

In 2022, Greta recruited over 100 experts to help write *The Climate Book*, a guide to climate change and how it can be addressed, including:

GEOPHYSICISTS
(study physics of the Earth, including climate)

OCEANOGRAPHERS
(study the physical qualities and life of the ocean)

METEOROLOGISTS
(study the weather and climate)

ECONOMISTS

ENGINEERS

MATHEMATICIANS

The book also explains and highlights the problem of 'greenwashing': when an organisation or company puts out misleading information about its supposedly 'green' activities to look environmentally responsible when it isn't.

HOW TO BE A CLIMATE WARRIOR

Are you ready to do your bit in helping to protect our planet? Here are some ideas...

Shop less

The planet's health depends on all of us shifting from unnecessary purchases to **sustainably sourcing** what we need and recycling it when we're done.

2/3RDS
of natural materials turned into products end up as waste!

Ditch the plastic
Half of all plastic produced is designed to be used only once and thrown away, which is wasteful and pollutes the environment. Carry a **reusable water bottle**, use **cloth shopping bags** and **recycle household waste**.

ONLY 10% of
plastic waste is recycled

PLASTIC

80 BILLION animals killed each year for food

Eat less meat

Raising and killing animals for meat and dairy consumption is one of the leading causes of many environmental problems. Livestock such as cows produce the greenhouse gas methane in their farts, which contributes to warming. Plus, forest and other natural habitat is destroyed to make room for farmland. Why not try **going veggie** or vegan on alternate days or **at least once a week**? Nowadays there are more meat-free options in supermarkets and it's easy to find plant-based recipes online.

Don't waste water

Climate change is causing droughts and water shortages around the world. Try to **use less water** by doing things like switching from **baths to showers**, **turning off the tap** when brushing your teeth or keeping a jug of **cold water in the fridge** rather than always filling a glass from the sink.

2-3 BILLION people experience water shortages at least 1 month a year

Grow a wild garden

Any outdoor space can be transformed into a haven for wildlife by **planting native flowers** that attract pollinating insects, **ditching pesticides** and creating a **compost heap**.

Think before you travel

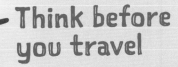

You can reduce your carbon footprint by taking fewer trips by plane and travelling via **train** or **bicycle** instead.

GLOSSARY

Atmosphere
The mixture of gases surrounding our planet.

Biosphere
The region above, on and below the Earth's surface where life can be found.

Citizens' assembly
When a group of people drawn from the public are brought together to discuss an important issue and reach an agreement or solution.

Climate
The weather conditions in an area over a long period of time.

Continent
A large continuous area of land, like Europe or Asia.

Economic
To do with trade, money and industry.

Ecosystem
A geographical area where animal and plant life interact with the environment.

Emissions
When something, like greenhouse gases, is released into the atmosphere.

Equity
When a situation or decision is fair to everyone involved.

Freeze-dried
When food is preserved by rapid freezing to remove its water content.

Glaciers
Slowly moving masses of ice made from compacted snow that has accumulated over many years.

Indigenous
The earliest known human inhabitants of an area.

Stigma
When a feeling of shame or embarrassment is wrongly associated with something, like a medical condition.

Turbine
A machine in which a rotor or wheel is turned by a fast-moving substance like water or gas to generate electricity.

Yacht
A medium-sized sailing boat used for travelling or racing.

First published 2023 by Button Books, an imprint of Guild of Master Craftsman Publications Ltd, Castle Place, 166 High Street, Lewes, East Sussex, BN7 1XU, UK. Copyright in the Work © GMC Publications Ltd, 2023. ISBN 978 1 78708 146 8. Distributed by Publishers Group West in the United States. All rights reserved. No part of this publication may be reproduced, stored in a retrieval system, or transmitted in any form or by any means without the prior permission of the publisher and copyright owner. While every effort has been made to obtain permission from the copyright holders for all material used in this book, the publishers will be pleased to hear from anyone who has not been appropriately acknowledged and to make the correction in future reprints. The publishers and authors can accept no legal responsibility for any consequences arising from the application of information, advice, or instructions given in this publication. A catalogue record for this book is available from the British Library. Senior Project Editor: Nick Pierce. Design: Tim Lambert, Dean Chillmaid. Illustrations: Alex Bailey, Matt Carr, Shutterstock. Colour origination by GMC Reprographics. Printed and bound in China.

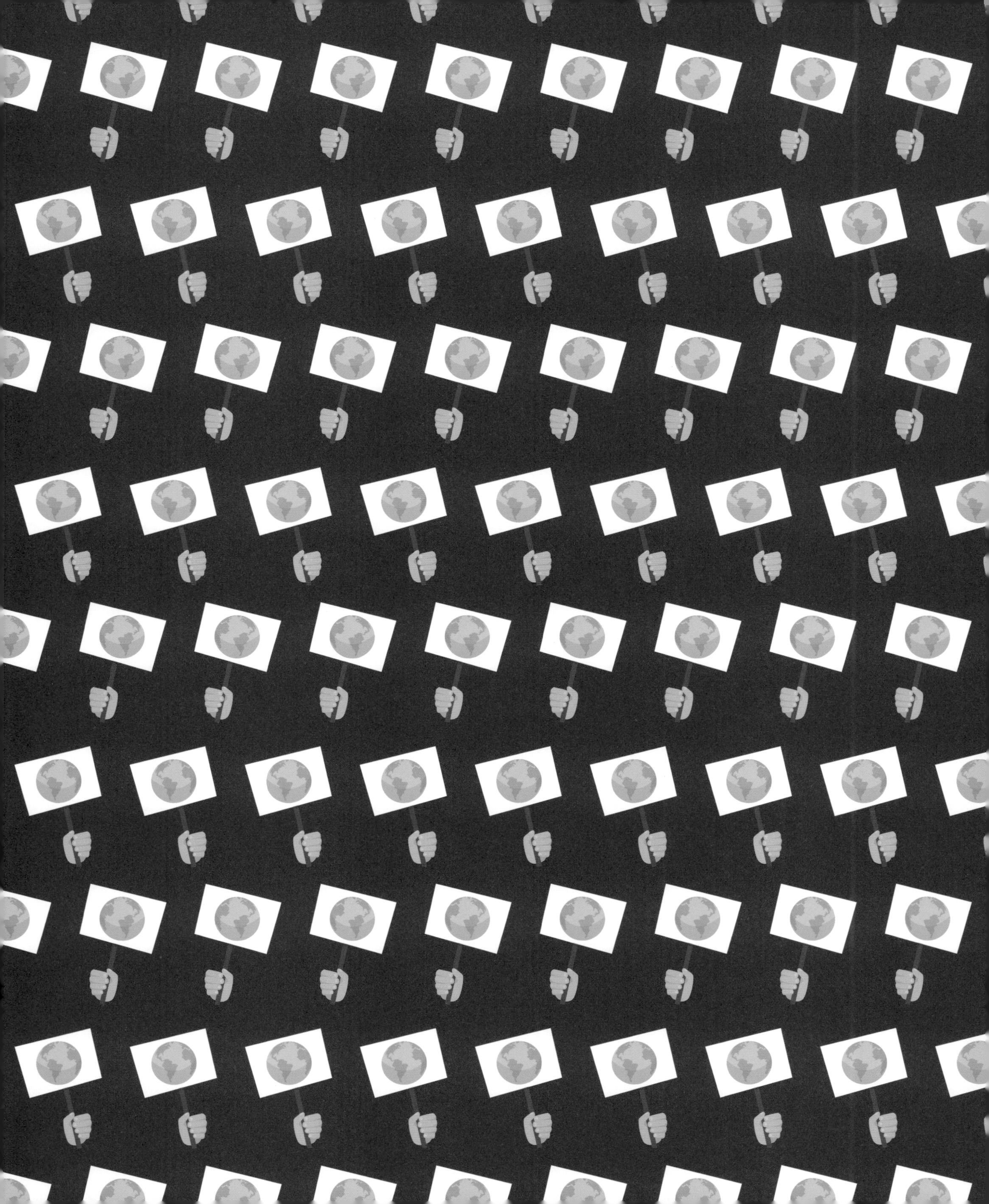

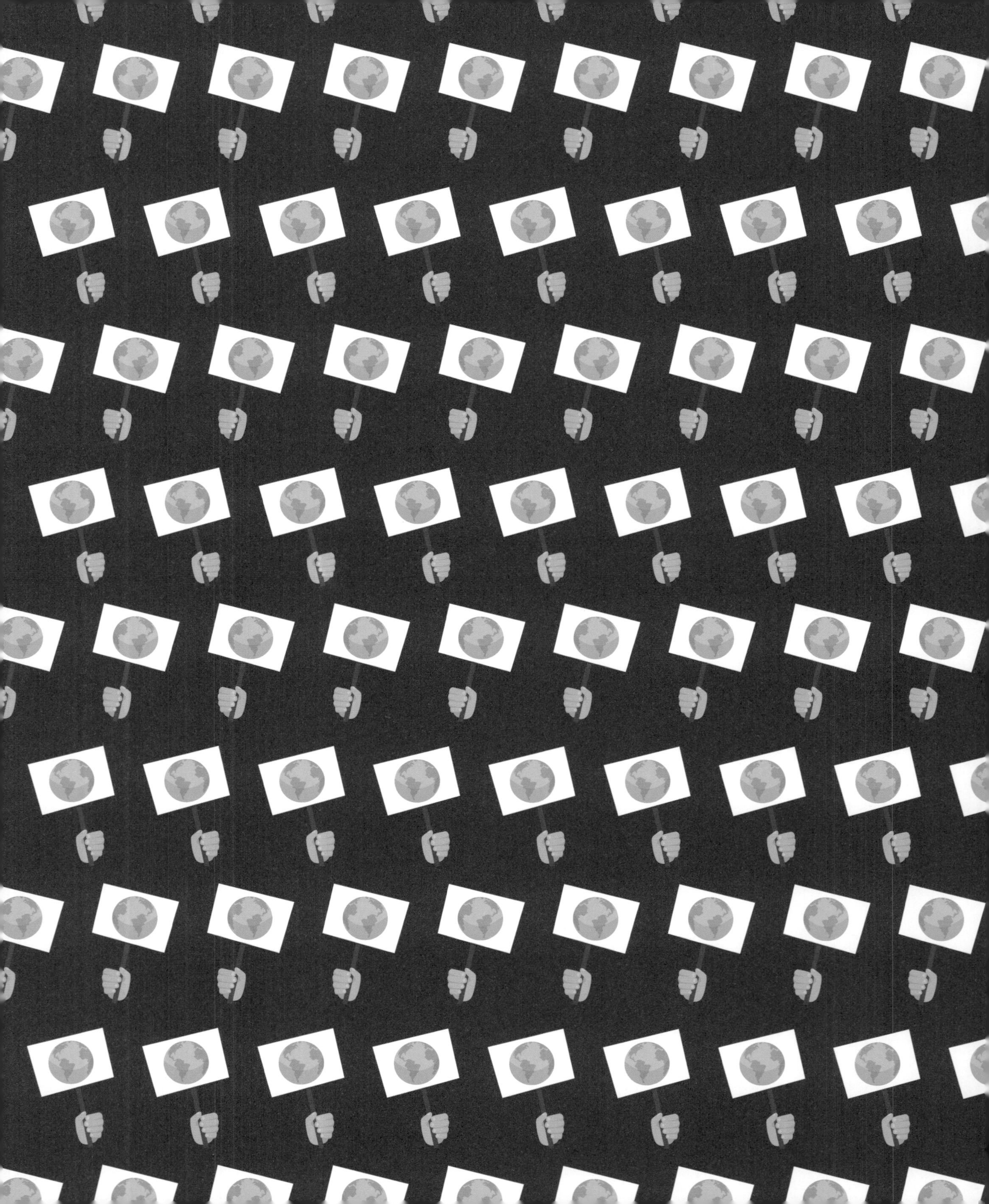